Guinness, My Pony

Erica Sloan Passman

Dedicated to Guinness

My Heart Horse (1994 to 2024)

Just missing his 30th birthday

We all love you, handsome boy.

Acknowledgments

Thank you to all these amazing people for being part of my life!

Especially my mommy!

Danny Campos

Michael Passman

Jennifer Khan And Shea

Susan 'Bridenstine' Gallagher

Marissa Butts

Monica Butts

Denise Johnson

Abby Lawson

Travis Lawson

Samantha Allison-Evans

Deanna Marcoux Mayrhofer

Stephanie Rucker

Emilee Spinelli

Shahram Amin

Susanne Greil

About the Author

Erica Sloan Passman is a Director of Customer Service and Logistics in the spirits and wine business with a dream of telling her story about her heart horse, Guinness.

Heightened by a lifelong love of fifteen years shared with the most incredible horse you could ever meet. Erica is not an author but worked hard to give Guinness everything he could possibly need and just really wanted to tell his story. She picked up her entire family and sold their dream home so that Guinness could retire in peaceful green fields and be close to her at home to ensure that he was getting the best care he needed.

Erica Sloan Passman captures the essence of loving a horse. Growing up in

Connecticut and moving to Texas, she finds that animals are the most loving, gentle, and caring.

She finds that they keep her emotionally and physically stable. When she's not spending time with her animals, she enjoys spending time with family and friends and having dinners out with great company.

Table of Contents

Guinness, My Pony 1
Meeting My New Mom 2
Heading to My New Home - Happy Acres 3
Heading to a Show Barn - Double B Equestrian 5
Trail Ride 8
Hunter Horse Shows 9
Dressage Horse Shows 11
Adventures 14
Bath Time 16
My Tail 18
Feeding and Bedtime 19
Veterinarian Visits 23
Farrier Days 26
Finally, A New Home of My Own 27
I'm Home on July 5th, 2019 29
Just Some Things That Happen Around Our Ranch 32
Meeting Baby Gunner 36
Life With My Brother 37
All the Kids in My Life 44
Finally, Retirement 46

Guinness My Pony

I was at a kill pen when a very special little girl from Greenville, Texas, came by and placed a bid on me! She won her bid and wanted to use me as a parade horse.

I did one parade with the little girl, and they found out I was afraid of flags, so they put me up for sale on Craigslist.

Meeting My New Mom

Little did I know I would be bought by the most loving family any animal could ever wish to live with.

It all started on a Sunday in August 2012 in Greenville, TX.

The weather was sunny and a bit windy.

I would never have guessed that I was going to meet an amazing lady named Erica, who would love and nurture me for the rest of my life and bring me back to be her lifelong horse partner.

My name was Yellow the day my mom and dad met me...but not for long though.

My name is now "Guinness," and I love my name.

Heading to My New Home - Happy Acres

I hauled to a farm named Happy Acres.

My new mom, Erica, was right there waiting to get me unloaded off the trailer. She was so excited to finally have her pony. She had been dreaming about it since she was a little girl.

We met so many wonderful people and horses at Happy Acres.

Here are just a few of the people who were so kind and caring and always around to lend a hand or just for great conversation!

Rachel Schwarz, Daphne McCann (rest her soul), Darby Peterson (owners - Don and Paulette Smith), and of course, Cory and Deb Pina.

Heading to a Show Barn - Double B Equestrian

We truly started riding every day, and sometimes I was a bit naughty, which made my mom a bit nervous, so she got me a trainer named Eduardo Salazar. Eduardo rode me every morning at five.

Eduardo worked at Double B Equestrian Center but was always so kind and helpful.

Mom and I just knew we could always count on him.

Mom would come in the evening to ride, and I was so tired from my morning ride with Eduardo that, yup, you guessed it, I was a good boy!

Mom was so happy, which, in turn, made me the best pony ever.

I always knew she was going to come in the early evening, and it gave me something to look forward to every day.

After riding, we would always go on a nice walk through the pasture, and then it would be bath time, supplements, and treats. Mom would then put me back in my stall across from my girlfriend Paulina and kiss me goodnight.

Mom and I met all kinds of horse friends and amazing people.

Just to list some of the folks who are still in our lives to this day.

Denise and Ken Johnson, Abby and Travis Lawson, Gloria Bayer, Celia Jones, Susan Gallagher, Denise Kennison, Pam and Mark Wilken and Marissa and Monica Butts.

I met so many new horsey friends who impacted my life daily.

Trail Rides

Finally, Mom and Dad bought me a new truck and trailer of my very own!

I knew that now that we had a truck and trailer of our own, Mom was going to start taking me on trial rides and horse shows!

On my first trail ride with our trainer Shahram and a huge herd of horses, Mom seemed a bit nervous when all the horses started trotting and cantering.

I wanted to keep up with the herd, but instead, I tripped, and Mom almost fell off. But I told her to just sit back and enjoy the ride...I will not let you fall. I will take care of you and keep you safe.

Hunter Horse Shows

Mom and I were both tense and flustered at my first hunter horse show, so I told her to just breathe; we would be okay.

I was spooked a little because I had never seen a judge stand before, but when the announcer came on and said we are starting the judging now at a walk, I perked my ears up, gave my mom a quick look and said, “Hang on, we are off!"

We ended up getting two-fifths and a fourth place, which was not bad for our first hunter horse show together.

Dressage Horse Shows

At my first dressage horse show, my trainer Emilee Spinelli rode me, and it was a super fun day; classes were early in the morning, so the heat of the Texas sun was not an issue. I won two first places in the classes I was signed up for.

Mom was so proud of me. She and Dad could not believe it. It was so exciting to have pictures taken of me, and people were amazed at how old I was and still in such good shape to compete.

When we returned to the barn, so many people had been waiting to congratulate us on our win.

I know many of them did not think I could do it. But, with all the practice and hard work we had been doing for months, it totally was noticed.

I went on to compete in more dressage shows and moved up to the walk, trot, and canter class...yup, you guessed it again, I won all the classes I was signed up for.

Just amazing, considering Mom always had to deal with negative feedback from others about my weight, my appearance, and my age.

But guess what? Mom, the trainer, and I showed all those disrespectful people. We worked twice as hard and accomplished so much together.

Mom really does not care whether I win or lose if I am having fun and trying.

She loves me!

Adventures

I am petrified of the flag cow (they call it cutting).

My mom's friend, Marissa Butts, used to come out to work with me a bit in front of the flag cow and lunged me for twenty-five minutes, and at the end, she petted my face with the flag cow.

We always finished on a good note, so as a reward, she loosened my girth and fed me some treats.

I do not think I will ever get over the flag cow fear, but maybe I will be a bit more relaxed near it.

I did love herding cows on Thursday nights. It's so much fun now that I am not scared of real cows.

We had the sweetest family named the Schreck's at the barn, two very lovely young ladies who let me play along and chase the cows back into the shoot while they practiced.

Bath Time

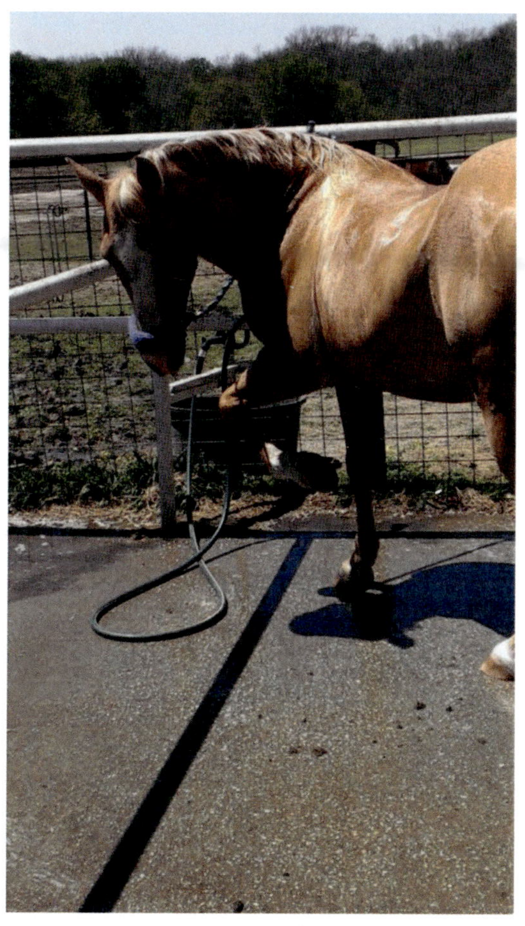

Bath days...I guess I was not very well-behaved during my bath. I moved around a lot, making it so hard for Mom.

But Mom always gets it done, and I'm clean and smell great.

I bet she is tired!

Don't worry, Mom, I will get better with this bath stuff.

My Tail

My mom spent a lot of time on my tail since the day she got me. She would braid it sometimes, and some days, she would take the braids out for a few days.

She always took pictures of me, especially when my tail was washed and brushed out. She always had serum on hand to make it smooth and silky.

She always said most girls would pay tons of money for hair like mine.

Feeding and Bedtime

On chilly days, my mom and dad would brave the cold weather and come to see me at least three times a day.

They would come to see me at six-thirty in the morning. They fed me breakfast and always brought warm boiling water. Checking on me to ensure I am warm, eating, and drinking before they head off to work.

Mom was not happy with me one morning. Luckily, it was a weekend morning when she and Dad came to the barn to feed and check on me as they always do every morning, but this time, my nose was sliced open. Mom had to clean and doctor me up a bit.

I know Mom and Dad are wondering how I got it...did I get bit by another horse last night? Did I cut it on something? Or...um. Lol, I'll never tell.

Darn, my mom is good and quick on her feet.

All clean now. Mom applied this cream called "Corona" all over my nose.

Anyway, my nose looks good.

Thank goodness.

Such a good mom. Oh, how she worries about me!

Mom and Dad head home for a bit. Mom returns to the barn around noon on the weekends, and we lunge for about thirty minutes.

Mom then brings me back to the cross ties, tacks me up, and rides.

Mom has a sweet friend whom she calls her mini-me. Mini-me rides quite often as well.

Especially if I am a bit frisky with Mom.

Mom always makes sure to untack me, groom me, and clean my feet before putting my blanket back on me if it's chilly.

I always get treats before Mom heads home.

Due to the cold weather, my mom always brings me warm water when she comes to feed me dinner.

I love it when Mom and Dad surprise me and come to see me at night after they have had their dinner out on the weekends.

I get to go out, graze, and have my Senior Heart treats.

Gosh, how they love me...yes, you could say I'm spoiled.

But I know my mom would not have it any other way.

Veterinarian Visits

I love it when my Vet from Parker Road Veterinary Hospital comes to visit. They come out twice a year to give me spring/fall shots to keep me healthy, and I usually have my blood sample taken so they can check my coggins.

On this one visit, Dr. Keren gave my mom some bad news...says I basically have broken my trachea and really will not be able to ride dressage anymore because I should not be holding my neck in a position that would hurt and suggested that it could be the reason why my nose is always snotty.

Dr. Keren drew blood to ensure I did not have an infection.

Doc says all my blood work is fantastic.

So yes, besides my trachea, snotty nose, and my old man teeth…I'm okay!

I guess we are going to take it a bit easy, hold off on lessons for a while, and just enjoy Mommy and me time.

Oh no…Mom called the vet again.

I have a lump on my belly and continuous diarrhea.

Mom does not play around when it comes to my health.

Dr. Keren is on his way.

Dr. Keren says I must wear a fly sheet because the sweat building up in my body has nowhere to go. It is accumulating under my belly, causing the lump.

Mom says I'm going to be fancy when my new fly sheet gets delivered to keep the flies away from my belly!

I need new fly boots too, to keep these darn flies from eating my legs and making me bleed. Mom is sending Dad to Dover Saddlery to buy me some on his way back home from work.

Thanks to my dad for my new fancy gray and navy lined fly boots.

Ah, so much better. Mom always knows what I need.

Farrier Days

I love my farrier, Freddy Martinez. He always knows exactly how to take care of my hoofs and makes them perfect, which in turn, makes my mom so very happy.

After getting my hooves shaped up, Mom usually takes me out for a walk around the big pasture.

Finally, A New Home of My Own

I am getting to come home on the weekends and watch all the work that is going into my new Morton barn.

So exciting! I just love my new yard.

I love to roll and trot around in it.

My human brother, Michael, just bought me a new water trough for outside, so I can get plenty of water when I'm home on the weekends.

I also love to help trim the trees.

Mom told me today that the barn doors are up, and they are working very hard to get my stall completed, so any day now, I will be moving home with my mom, dad, brother Mike, and my dog, Kanan.

Oh, one more thing I have two very nice mares that live right next door to me: Boo and Cheena.

I'm Home on July 5th, 2019

Getting to know my brother, Kanan, a bit better.

Yeah, I think he is okay now that he is not a puppy anymore.

He loves to hang out with me on the other side of the fence sometimes.

We even take naps together.

He also loves to watch me get groomed and take my baths.

Mom says I can only eat grass in certain areas because the Morton workers are still working.

But guess what? I do not listen very well, and I go under the rope that Dad put up and wander around the entire pasture that is just for me.

I love being free!

I'm not supposed to be in the barn alone.

I'm very nosey!

Finally, we have power in the new barn.

Mom and Dad worked in my tack room tonight. They both look sweaty.

I just love being home!

Getting to be free out in the pasture all the time and just knowing my mom is always around is kind of comforting to me.

I just love it when the sun is shining, and I get to hang out with my new mare horse buddies and just mosey around walking in the pasture.

Being out of my stall on nice days is the sweetest feeling.

Yup, Mom has started to ride me bareback out in the pasture for only fifteen minutes, but she has made me do all kinds of turns and stretches.

Did she forget, I want to retire now?

Love seeing Mom multiple times a day.

Our ranch is now officially called GQuest!

My mom's friend, Evelyn Minnick, had a beautiful sign made up with our name so we could hang it in our barn.

Just Some Things That Happen Around Our Ranch

My mom tried to get me a new friend. His name was Lance.

I did not like Lance going anywhere near my mare friends on the other side of the fence.

Lance spent the weekend, and on Monday, my brother Michael was heading to work and ran into the house to let my mom know I was bleeding from my nose and my side cheek was cut open.

Seems we got into a little scuffle.

Well, my mom was not having it as she knew I was not happy with this new friend so the first thing she did was call the owner and tell them we cannot keep

Lance for you, and we need to find him another home.

Then she called the vet!

Thank goodness for good friends who helped Mom take care of me and were able to haul Lance to his new home.

I know Mom felt bad about calling Lance's owners because she was trying to help them.

She did give them all the things she had bought over the weekend for him.

Lead Ropes, halter, feed, and hay!

Don't worry about me. The vet came, and I had twenty stitches on my cheek, and eventually, my nose stopped bleeding.

Well, you have to remember, I am old and set in my ways!

My brother Michael's girlfriend, Raven Owens, even jumps on me bareback for a quick ride sometimes.

I have my babysitter, Monica Butts, who comes out seven days a week to clean my stall and play with me, especially Monday through Friday when Mom is at work.

She takes lots of photos of me and sends them to Mom so she can see that I am happy, feeling okay, and enjoying my day.

It gets really cold sometimes, but my mom comes outside to hang with me so I am not lonely and makes sure I have plenty of hay and my blankets are on properly.

I cannot stand the cold, and I very much dislike rain. I want it to be about

75 degrees and sunny, with the grass green and flowers blooming.

Ugh, it's either a blanket or fly spray here.

Mom says I might be getting a new friend next weekend.

We are rescuing her.

She was found on a major highway.

Thanks to some very special ladies taking care of her, they approached my mom to take her.

We will call her Tanqueray!

Our kitty, Tanqueray, loves to sleep on my shavings in the corner of the tack room.

Mom found a snake in my stall; why is our kitty not doing her job?

Meeting Baby Gunner

May 26th, 2020!

Yes, I have a new baby brother.

His name is Gunner!

He is so tiny, so Mom and Dad are keeping us apart right now.

Slowly, they are introducing us to each other.

Gosh, he is lucky. He gets milk three times a day!

We are starting to gradually spend more time together out in the pasture without baby Gunner having to be on a lead line.

I do not mind, if he goes over to see my mare friends on the other side of the fence, as he is just a tiny baby, after all.

Life With My Brother

He follows me everywhere I go.

He just wants me to be like his daddy!

This kid will not leave me alone, even when Mom is trying to shower me.

I think this kid loves me!

He is next to me in the morning, noon, and night.

Yes, Gunner even drinks fresh water with me after Dad cleans all the troughs on the weekends.

We even have matching blankets now.

Ugh, I thought I was retired!

But, since my brother Gunner is trying to learn to be a good horse, Mom works with me too.

Well, guess it's good for me!

Have I told you how much I love my mom, dad, brother Mike, Kanan, Tanqueray, and baby Gunner?

Life is not easy anymore!

Training days are crazy.

My brother Gunner is a nut.

It's hot out this week, so Mom and Dad are training Gunner to load in a trailer so I can get to rest.

Ah, finally, I get to rest under my tree while I watch baby Gunner napping.

It's so very peaceful.

I like to go into Gunner's stall, so he tends to sleep under the awning of the barn.

I get to spend a lot of one-on-one time with Mom as she takes me off the property to take walks down the street.

Gunner has a trainer, who comes out every Saturday (Mark Tarver) and works with him and Mom on ground manners.

I just watch and laugh as that boy has so much to learn!

He is coming along quite nicely, and Mom is learning a lot and practicing all the things she learns with me.

Ya wonder why? Because I listen, and if she can do it with me, she should be able to do it with Gunner.

So, we took baby Gunner to a new trainer off-site today and watched this trainer, Gloria Bayer, at Kavallerie Farm ground drive him.

So, I guess Mom will be practicing with me now.

Yes, she practiced today. She is pretty good, but it's easy if you have a horse that does it well.

LOL, that would be me!

Baby Gunner fears the fireworks that are going off.

I am trying to hold in my fear and teach him that it is okay. I am here, and I will look after him.

Gunner now must wear a fly mask too, just like me.

Ya know, it protects us from the sun too.

Lake days.

It was so peaceful...me and my dad.

Oh yes.

Baby Gunner and Mom too.

I'm not sure Mom had so much fun, especially because baby Gunner did not behave so well.

My mom loves me so much.

Mom kept telling Gunner while riding me.

This is the goal.

We have another trainer, Amy Maas, at Amiable Horsemanship, who now comes out to our barn three days a week.

I watch her very closely as she works with baby Gunner.

I'm constantly worried about him!

I have a quick conversation with Gunner before the trainer, and Mom come out to catch him for his workout!

Trying to tell and advise him that if you are a good boy...you will be done quickly and get nice treats.

He looks at me as if saying, "Oh well, I do not know what I'm talking about."

Guess because Gunner is learning how to lift his feet over trot poles.

I must now get my exercise too!

The trainer has an amazing dog (Sydney). She keeps all the squirrels and rabbits out of our yard and away from me.

After Gunner's lessons are over, it is back to babysitting him.

A new trainer for Gunner, his name is Tom Hall and he is helping my mom so much with groundwork and riding. I'm very impressed with him too; he is making Gunner look very fancy.

All the Kids in My Life

Thank you to all the little, young adults, and, yes, my mom, who are all so very special in my life and love me so much.

All these special individuals come over and ride me, groom me, and give amazing treats.

I have to say, I feel the love!

I was even in a wedding shoot!

I'm telling you, these lovely people come from far away just to see me!

A special thanks to a little girl who chose to take up horseback riding all because of me!

Shea! That would be you!

Thank you to all these amazing people for being part of my life and sharing your littles with me!

Jennifer Khan, Susan 'Bridenstine' Gallagher, Denise Johnson, Abby and Travis Lawson, Deanna Marcoux Mayrhofer, Stephanie Rucker, and Emilee Spinelli.

Finally, Retirement

I have started to get PEMF Therapy once a month on Sundays. RM Performance – PEMF Therapies, LLC, I receive full Body Maintenance Massages and Full Body Dual PEMF sessions with Rachael Kernan. This helps me to increase circulation, increase my range of motion, reduce stress and tension, and much more.

Sometimes, now, I get terrible belly aches, so my mom walks me until I poop at least twice.

I know she prays a lot that I will be ok.

My poor mom.

The vet just left because Mom doesn't like to take any chances when it comes to me.

I had to have shots of Banamine and a hose up my nose so that the vet could put oil and warm water down the hose from my nose into my belly. Yes, the vet checked in my rear, too.

I know my mom will be up all night...I'm tired now, but she keeps coming out to walk me every hour.

I'm sure she will not be sleeping tonight. She will be watching me on the cameras she and Dad installed so they can always see what I am up to.

Have I told you how much I love my mommy?

I now get to do whatever I want to. I love spending time in Kanan's yard with him grazing. I even taught him how to graze.

Mom always seems to have the camera on her phone out. She cannot resist taking pictures of me.

Yes, I am a bit spoiled, but I've earned it.

Now that I am twenty-nine years old.

I get showered on warm days, get to hang in Kanan's yard, roll every morning to stretch my body, and little kids come out to sit on my back and walk around either in the pasture or the indoor arena. My niece comes from CT to visit me once a year and rides me bareback. She also helps Mom feed and take care of me.

Mom still gets on my back to walk me around. Guess I still need to do some exercise!

I take a lot of naps, get fed so well twice a day, and am free to walk around our pastures as I please!

All in all, this has been a terrific life meeting my mom and my family.

I am truly blessed to be able to retire at home on my property in my barn, which was built especially for me to be with my family!

I would not change one thing about my life with this terrific family who saved me fifteen years ago from Greenville.

They care for me, love me, and treat me like royalty!

Mom always says – I am her best boy and a gentle giant!

Made in United States
Orlando, FL
03 June 2024

47491725R00033